Technology That Changed the World

The Television
Window to the World

Joanne Mattern

The Rosen Publishing Group's
PowerKids Press™
New York

Published in 2003 by The Rosen Publishing Group, Inc.
29 East 21st Street, New York, NY 10010

First Edition

Book Design: Michael DeLisio

Photo Credits: Cover © Craig Orsini/Index Stock Imagery, Inc.; pp. 5, 6–7 © Hulton-Deutsch Collection/Corbis; pp. 8, 9, 14, 16 © Bettmann/ Corbis; p. 11 © Getty Images; pp. 12, 13 © Culver Pictures; p. 15 © Hulton/Archive/Getty Images; p. 17 (top) © AP/Wide World Photos; p. 17 (bottom) © TimePix; p. 18 © Lou Jones/Index Stock Imagery, Inc.; p. 19 (top) © SuperStock, Inc.; p. 19 (bottom) © Paul A. Souders/Corbis; p. 20 © Reuters NewMedia Inc./Corbis; p. 21 © Leng/Leng/Corbis

Library of Congress Cataloging-in-Publication Data

Mattern, Joanne, 1963–
Television : window to the world / Joanne Mattern.
   p. cm. — (Technology that changed the world)
Summary: Presents information on television, including its invention, history, how it works, and how it has affected people's lives.
Includes bibliographical references and index.
ISBN 0-8239-6493-0 (library binding)
1. Television—Juvenile literature. [1. Television.] I. Title.
TK6640 .M38 2003
621.388—dc21
                                            2002000507

Contents

The First Television Inventors

Many discoveries and experiments in the late 1800s led to the invention of the television. In 1884, Paul Nipkow invented a way to send images, or pictures, over long distances. He placed a disk with special holes in front of a brightly lit picture. As the disk spun around, different parts of the picture could be seen. With each complete turn of the disk, the whole picture was seen.

Nipkow got the idea of sending pictures over long distances while living in Berlin, Germany. His family lived far away and he missed them. Nipkow wished there was a way they could see each other.

Inventors in England and the United States used the Nipkow disk to make early televisions. In 1928, John Logie Baird used a Nipkow disk to broadcast, or send, television pictures from London, England, to New York City.

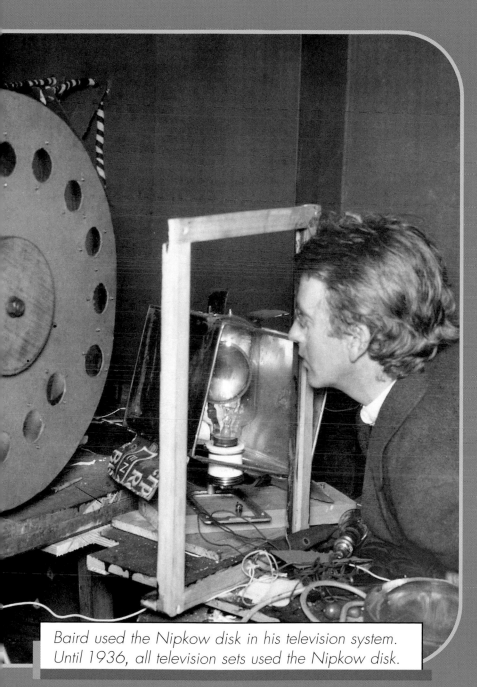

Baird used the Nipkow disk in his television system.
Until 1936, all television sets used the Nipkow disk.

Other inventors found a different way to send pictures. In 1923, Vladimir Zworykin *(VLA-duh-mihr ZWAR-ih-kuhn)* invented the first successful television camera tube and an early model of the television picture tube. A television picture tube allowed pictures to be seen more clearly. In 1927, Philo Farnsworth invented an electronic television camera tube.

Zworykin was known as "the father of television." Here, he holds one of the television picture tubes he invented.

Farnsworth was a teenager when he had the idea for a television system that was better than the ones that were being used at the time. Here, he checks one of his early television sets.

How Television Works

A television camera records an image and then breaks up the picture into thousands of tiny parts. Each part is turned into an electrical signal. Television stations use large antennas to send the signals through the air. A small antenna in a television set picks up the signals and sends them to the picture tube in the television set. The picture tube puts the signals together, making the picture appear on the screen.

Now You Know

The first U.S. television station began broadcasting in Schenectady, New York, on May 10, 1928.

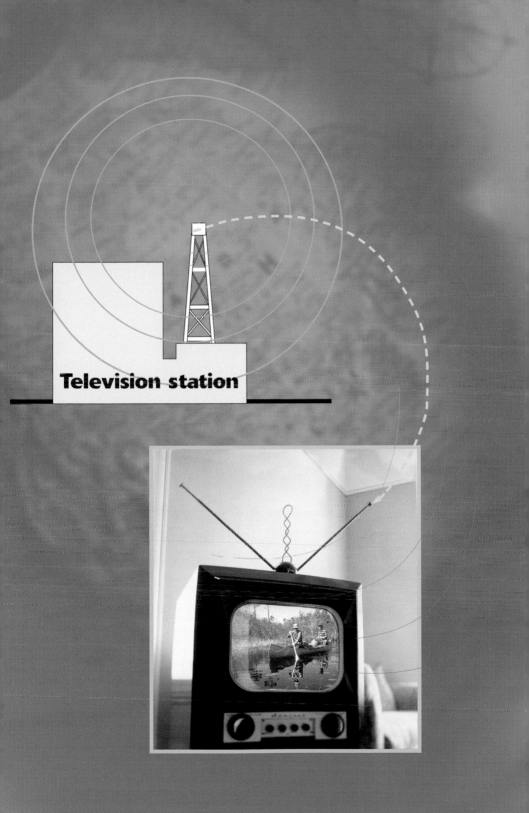

Television station

Television and the World

The invention of television changed the way people lived. People were able to get news and entertainment quickly by viewing television programs. Regular television broadcasts began throughout the United States in 1939.

Early televisions were large, but had very small screens.

During World War II (1939–1945), all television programs went off the air. During that time, radios were the main way that people got their news and entertainment.

Work on making better televisions stopped during World War II. Instead, businesses made tools and machines that would help the United States win the war.

After World War II, the use of television grew very quickly. Many of the first television programs were broadcast live, and all of them were seen in black and white only. The most popular programs were comedy shows, westerns, variety shows, and game shows.

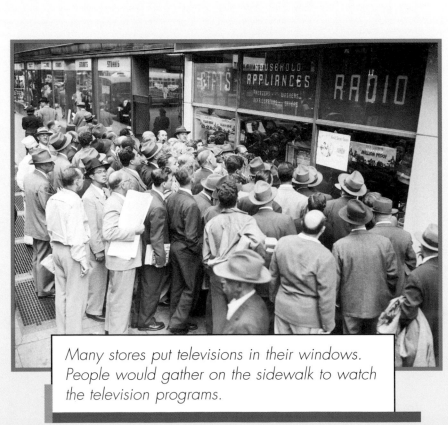

Many stores put televisions in their windows. People would gather on the sidewalk to watch the television programs.

The First Five Countries to Have Television

Country	Year
United Kingdom (England)	1936
United States	1939
USSR (Russia)	1939
France	1948
Brazil	1950

In the 1950s, television technology was made better. Television signals got stronger. Television pictures and sounds became clearer. Television screens were made larger. In 1954, television programs could be seen in color.

The growth of television let people around the world see important events as they were happening. During the 1960s, people watched news about the Civil Rights movement and the Vietnam War. Sometimes, the ways people thought and acted were changed by what they saw on television.

In 1960, people watched Richard Nixon (right) and John F. Kennedy (left) speak about why they wanted to be president of the United States.

The Beatles first appeared on U.S. television on The Ed Sullivan Show on February 9, 1964. Over 73 million Americans watched the Beatles sing.

About 720 million people watched astronaut Neil Armstrong walk on the Moon on July 20, 1969.

Adding to Television

In the 1970s, cable television and the home videotape recorder made television even more popular. Cable television gave people more television programs to watch. Videotape recorders allowed people to record, or tape, one show while watching another. People could also rent or buy videos to watch movies at home on their televisions.

Cable box

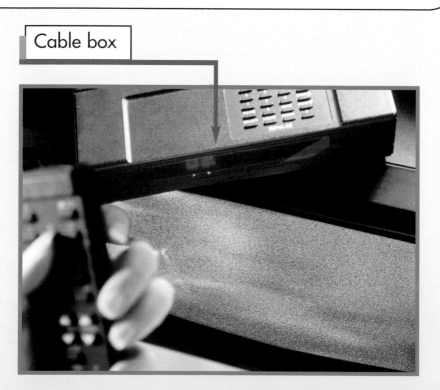

Videotape recorder

Satellite dish

During the 1990s, satellite dishes became popular. Satellites in space receive signals from television stations. The satellites make the signals stronger and then send them to satellite dishes on people's homes.

19

Television Today

Today, there are more than 1,500 television stations in the United States. Americans own over 219 million television sets. Television is more popular than ever before.

People can watch television to see the U.S. government at work.

Time Line

1884:   Paul Nipkow invents the Nipkow disk.

1923:   Vladimir Zworykin invents an early television camera and television picture tube.

1927:   Philo Farnsworth invents an electronic television camera tube.

1939:   Regular television broadcasts begin in the United States.

1954:   Television broadcasts are shown in color.

1969:   People all over the world watch Neil Armstrong walk on the Moon.

1970s: The home videotape recorder and cable television are used by television viewers.

1990s: Satellite dishes become popular with television users.

Most Americans will spend about 1,600 hours watching television each year.

Glossary

antenna (an-**tehn**-uh) a metal rod or wire or a dish-shaped object used for sending or receiving electric signals

broadcast (**brawd**-kast) to send out radio or television signals; a radio or television show

Civil Rights movement (**sihv**-uhl **ryts moov**-muhnt) events that took place during the 1950s and 1960s that worked toward getting equal rights for all citizens of the United States

electrical (ih-**lehk**-truh-kuhl) having to do with power that is used to make light, heat, or motion

electronic (ih-lehk-**trahn**-ihk) containing special parts that control the flow of electricity

picture tube (**pihk**-chuhr **toob**) a tube on which the picture appears in a television

popular (**pahp**-yuh-luhr) liked by many people

programs (**proh**-gramz) radio or television shows

satellite dishes (**sat**-l-yt **dihsh**-uhz) dish-shaped objects that receive signals sent by satellites (spacecraft that go around the earth) and then send the signals to a television

signal (**sihg**-nuhl) an electrical wave that sends sounds and pictures to radios and televisions

Resources

Books

Television
by Catherine Chambers
Heinemann (2001)

Television: What's Behind What You See
by W. Carter Merbreier and Linda Capus Riley
Farrar, Straus and Giroux (1995)

Web Sites

Due to the changing nature of Internet links, PowerKids Press has developed an online list of Web sites related to the subjects of this book. This site is updated regularly. Please use this link to access the list:

http://www.powerkidslinks.com/tcw/tlvs/

Index

Word Count: 474

Note to Librarians, Teachers, and Parents

If reading is a challenge, Reading Power is a solution! Reading Power is perfect for readers who want high-interest subject matter at an accessible reading level. These fact-filled, photo-illustrated books are designed for readers who want straightforward vocabulary, engaging topics, and a manageable reading experience. With clear picture/text correspondence, leveled Reading Power books put the reader in charge. Now readers have the power to get the information they want and the skills they need in a user-friendly format.